Woman on the Terrace

Woman on the Terrace

POEMS BY MOON CHUNG-HEE

Translated by
Seong-kon Kim and Alec Gordon

WHITE PINE PRESS / BUFFALO, NEW YORK

White Pine Press
P.O. Box 236, Buffalo, New York 14201
www.whitepine.org

Cover: *September* by Chang Won-sang *(1926–1982)*.
Ink and light color on Korean paper
Used by permission of the
National Museum of Contempory Art, Seoul, Korea.

First Edition

Publication of this book was made possible with public funds from
the New York State Council on the Arts, a State Agency,
and by generous grants from the
Korea Literature Translation Institute
and the Sunshik Min Endowment for the Advancement of Korean Literature
at the Korea Institute, Harvard University.

Printed and bound in the United States of America.

13-digit ISBN 978-1-893996-86-1

Library of Congress Control Number: 2007937846

Contents

PART II

Part III

PART IV

Part V

Prelude

A Poet's Perennial Epigraph

Such a long journey,
on unfamiliar roads—

but along the way, I found God.

Part I

This Autumn Day

I'm my own God this autumn day.
With all the words I have, I'm the God of my own.

Autumn falls silently between the stars,
and between you and me.

As God's primordial sword
finely thrusts and stabs,
everything, in solitude, glows.
Each and every autumn leaf,
those free, solitary birds—
so hard to render in human speech.
So hard to write a poem this autumn day—
as hard as moving a mountain!

Being myself, I'm already complete.
Birds, stars, flowers, leaves, mountains, clothes,
food, home, earth, blood, body, water, fire, dream, island—
and you and I,
we are already poetry.

On this autumn day, I am
at last, the God of my own.

Muffler

When we walk, my arm around her shoulders,
people whisper that we're a great couple,
but I'm merely a wing covering her wounds,
a bandage wrapped around her pain.
Dauntless as a redwood tree—
doesn't she need the protection
afforded by an Arabian woman's chador?
Soon I may be a prison for her,
like a molting skin
to be quickly tossed aside.

No! Even if it's not windy
we walk, my arm around her.
People whisper we're a great couple,
but I'm merely her banner raised in battle—
a matador's cape proclaiming war against the world.

Dusk descends like warm memories.
Her unforgettable warmth—
oh, unforgettable warmth!

Encounter with a Shrimp

Not having the heart to cut it into pieces
I quietly put the knife down.
On a plane bound for Paris
the crescent-shaped shrimp on my tray
reminds me of my peninsula home.
Way up in the sky, at immense height,
almost in the dreamy Milky Way,
what fate brought us to meet—
a creature of the sea
and a creature of the land?
Perhaps our encounter was predestined
by some hidden thread of fate
silently weaving a dream from clouds,
from your earnest yearning and my eager passion.
So instead of a knife and fork,
I pressed my soft, warm lips
to that naked pink body—
oh, my beloved Gyunwoo!

Memories of Yulpo

My mother took me to the sea when I was young
not to show me the salty blue water
but to show me the life wriggling on the dark tidal flats.
After the tide suddenly turned and raced from the shore
there—there was the strength of all living things
scuttling and fluttering despite the danger.

Why do people kneel to reach for food?
Why do they bend so deeply over?
Why are tidal flats full of living things so bare?

My mother took me to the sea when I was young
not to let me hear the sound of the tide
but to show me the sad, diligent hands
that ferret for food on the flats,
people genuflecting as if to saints,
and against a backdrop of nesting waterfowl,
the port aglow in sunset's mottled light.

Moon

Today is a beautiful day—meaninglessly
crystal clear, like a mirror.
On a piece of paper,
instead of writing a poem, I'm drawing a yellow moon.
I'm tired of those poems,
full of dishonesty, exaggeration, pretense, and bragging.
Tired of those poems about flowers, mountains and birds..
Tired even of anger, happiness, apleasure and love..
I'm drawing a moon on a piece of paper,
clipping it out with scissors, and hanging it on the gate.
It will be a yellow lantern, rather than a red one.
Since you call me *Moon*,
the moon will be my nameplate on the gate.
Indeed, I am literature, I am the moon.
I'm floating, yearing for you like a lantern
shedding light on the agonies of the world.
Why not be a red beacon
for those who, destitute and lonely,
roam the streets in search of love?
They may enter the gate free of charge.

Today is beautiful day—meaninglessly
crystal clear, like a mirror.

Earth

I envy most the name earth.
Whisper its name—earth, earth, earth.
From deep in my heart
I can feel my tears—
my eyes are wet.

I didn't see earth as the start
and destination of life.
I once saw an earth-loving potter
who caressed it day and night
until an exquisite moon was born,
and I saw someone sow a handful of seeds in its bosom
and harvest a heap of grain when the season came.
Since it's the labor of the earth
farmers, in modesty, call it farming
rather than a miracle.

Still I envy most the name earth.
Whisper the name—earth, earth, earth.
From deep down in the well of my tears,
I hear the echo of a sad, beautiful life—
the sound of heaven scooping itself
from the well it created on earth.

Letter from a Daughter

Father, here I am, still alive
after slashing the drum that protected my country
with the dagger hidden in my bosom.
What I slashed was not the magic drum
which beats at the sight of enemies.
It was my own destiny.
Father, I tore your country apart with my own hands.
Trembling with fear and unassuageable guilt,
blind to the future, I threw myself into the task.
Then, I was like the raging wind.
Prince Hodong was full of grace, like the moon,
but it was not for him that I tore the drum apart.
My love was like a helpless flower
blooming on the steep and giddy cliff of war.
How could love bring me only disaster?
When I wielded the dagger in the air to slash the drum,
disguised in a pitch-black mask,
I realized the dark despair
that makes even stars tremble
was mine alone.

A Party for the Blind

All the people I met were blind.
They lived with their hands groping in air,
constantly tapping the earth with their white canes.
Foggy alleys seemed endless drenched with rain.
There was an airport by the highway,
but no-one could fly far anyway.
I often wondered if the party for the blind
would be held on the highway to the palace.
Meanwhile, the lotus bloomed and faded away.
No news about Simchong had reached me yet.
It was so dark. I wondered if it were a dream,
but it was reality.
It appeared to be a desert, but it was my home.
Where is the palace?
All the people I met were
heading for the party for the blind.

Between Clocks

This morning I woke to a broken clock.
It brushes its teeth,
has its breakfast,
and gets older.

Somewhere out there
there may be a clock pointing to the correct time.
I want a clock like that.

I watch CNN.
Embarrassed, the network hurriedly sends a reporter
to the scene of the broken clock.
Trying to flatter me and rubbing their hands
they point a gun at the clock.
To describe the people who try to fix broken clocks,
CNN uses words like "communication" and "diplomacy."

In the end we all live differently,
so it's impossible to synchronize all the watches on earth.
Between you and me, there's always a different time zone.
Walking with a broken clock
I stop at the crossroad to look up at the clock tower.
Which clock is correct, I don't know.

Clocks are ageless
and drifting toward the unknown.

Tree School

I'm going to learn the art of aging from trees.
Every year I grow older as age accrues—
henceforth no more simple additions.
I'd rather engrave my age inside me, like a tree.

When I walk among evergreen trees,
when a branch lightly brushes my shoulder,
when autumn gently places its hand on me,
when his "I love you!" penetrates my heart,
when I say "Smile," capturing the moment
against a wooded background,
trees already grown, without revealing their age,
fortify the ancient temple—
like young trees abounding with hope.

I'm going to learn the art of aging from trees,
engraving the passing years inside of me—
being, for sure, more green and lush next year.

Love Document

Love often nests on forbidden ground.
Happiness is more likely a rickety house
but don't worry—
even before the demolition crew arrives
it will become an empty place,
like the wandering nomads' camp.

Often making an illegal U-turn,
love is built on violation and secrecy,
but it doesn't need to file a report—
perhaps that's why poetry was invented.
I've begun to think of this tonight.

Where on the earth do all the people live?
Suddenly this city's peace seems phony.
Would that I could gloriously fall
into a solemn love affair.
I wish I could blindly push it to extremes.
Why do people wail with throat-tight sorrow?
True love, true pain, and true hope
are not recorded in any document.
I've begun to think of this tonight.

Love of Fire

Where can we find passion in life?
Although the wretched fall is inevitable,
fire has always made the world beautiful.
Oh, Fire!
Flap your thousand wings,
shoot down the stars,
soar toward the sky.
If it weren't for you,
how could we dream of transcendent eternity?
If it weren't for your burning heart,
could we even think of a love
that challenges annihilation?

Girl Urinating

Oh daughter, refrain from indiscreetly crouching to pee.
Do it gracefully, squatting beneath a green tree.
Listen to the gentle sound of water permeating earth—
the warm river running from your exquisite body—
dancing to nature's flowing rhythms.
Listen to the sound of the green grass growing,
to the harmony of you and nature becoming one.

Occasionally, you may want to pee
against a rock to express your disdain—
but wait!—like a ritual, gently lift your skirt
and let your full moonflower gently brush the earth,
listen to the sound of you and earth merging
as the warm river in your body seeps into the dirt.
Tune into the nature's rhythmical melody.
Be privy to the applause of all verdant life.
Oh, my dear girl!

Detour

Do not approach the stone Buddha
whose eyes and nose are gone.
Only its traces remain.
No longer a Buddha,
it's returning to perfection,
it's returning to stone.
Karma carved eyes and nose
in this Inhak temple courtyard
a thousand years ago.
Buddha's prison is sacred and profound.
Time does not exist
in the natural process
of returning to uncarved stone.
Don't clasp your hands in prayer in vain.
Let the word "perfection" be enough.

Talking to My Naked Body

Taking my morning shower,
I talk to my naked body:

"Don't follow me.
I'm a poet,
but you don't have to be.
Yesterday I aged three years.
Suddenly it's happened—
I'm a hundred-year-old fox.
Oh, naked body!
I pray you'll be three years younger each day.
You've betrayed me so many times.
Against my wishes, you got wrinkled and fat.
You met men while I silently wrote poetry.
Even so, please stay naked.
Spend time in bed with a poppy in your hair
rather than behind your desk.
Oh, my windmill, my chapel."

Midnight

Lightning struck me at midnight,
penetrating straight to my heart.
It took my ruby-like scarlet sins
and scattered them across the dark sky.

It's hard to believe lightning
from the mountains
helps the bright sun
care for the green forest and the birds
during the day—
the very lightning that at midnight
struck my heart.

The lightning took those crystal-clear rubies
from my trembling heart
and scattered them across the sky.

Tomorrow morning there will be a prisoner
in my bed, a prisoner who all night long
tried to write a sad, profound confession.

Part II

Woman on the Terrace

The woman smoking a cigarette,
holding it between long-nailed fingers,
her eyes sunken—
like an archer who's just shot her last arrow.
The woman with wrinkled lips pouring down red wine,
her hair unkempt.
Marriage came easy to her; divorce even easier.
But that was fine by her.
At times she was lonely. So be it.
She didn't know the flower's name.
So many scars and confessions.
Vanished embraces; heartbeats that disappeared like the wind,
sentimental and mundane.
But her life was full of such pain and agony.
The woman on the terrace smiled, shrugged her shoulders
gazing at the backs of people
who avoided her, made their asinine jokes,
afraid her thorns might prick.
I'd never met her before
but she looked familiar—
omnipresent!

From Poetry to a Tree

Why are you standing there, Tree?

Come, leave the ground
and spill blood.
Take out your green heart and reveal it to me.
Sing the secret of your agelessness
like I do, in words.
Though I can't understand your song,
it's melodious and exhuberant,
more radiant than the sorrow
hiding in my poems.
Those songs
you sang while alone, extracting sap
from deep underground.
Come, leave the ground
and let me hear them.

Why are you standing there, Tree?

Letter from the Airport

Please, leave me alone for a year, my dear.
I'm on sabbatical from our marriage
We've come a long way since our wedding vows
to stay together for better or for worse
until death do us part.

We settled at a desert oasis,
rooted deeply and grew branches.
But please, for one year, don't try to follow me.
Soldiers needs to take leave.
Workers need a holiday.
As quiet scholars go on sabbatical for renewal,
I now take my well-earned leave.
So please, don't look for me for a year, my dear.
I'll return when I've found myself.

The Age of Success

What shall I do? I've become rich!
Plenty of food in the 'fridge,
tons of brand new dresses in the closet—
happiness is everywhere!
Chinese food delivered instantly via phone,
a comfy car carrying me here and there—
if I take the wheel, I can go anywhere.
At last, I'm successful!
When I abandon poetry, all misery will fade away.
When I buy a pearl necklace, everything will be okay.
No more twilights and green pastures in my heart.
No more tears more clear than morning dew.
No more solitude, secretly, like an alley cat, creeping in
to announce the bankruptcy of poetry.
Shall I start this business of happiness?
Shall I madly dart, driving a powerful car
fast as a speeding bullet, into the dark city?

Husband

Neither my father nor my brother,
he's the man standing somewhere in between.
Someone who is closest, yet so remote.
When I'm suffering from insomnia
I'm inclined to ask for his advice—
oops! anything but that!
So I silently turn away from him in bed.
Sometimes my enemy,
other times, the only man on earth
who holds my children so dear.
So I make dinner for him again,
this man I've dined with so many times,
this man who taught me how to fight.

Family Photo: Women on a Snowy Day

The women in our old family photos...

The woman not honored by a monument
for the noble deed of serving her starving husband her flesh.
The woman not enshrined for the bravery
of severing her hand when it was grabbed by a Japanese soldier.
The woman not remembered for
remaining a faithful widow since the age twenty,
spending so many lonely, restless nights
burning her thigh with a hot iron to cool off.

My big-eyed widowed grandmother
who'd been so beautiful
she was kidnapped by a secret admirer one night.
My aunt—pregnant before her wedding,
who'd had to hide her large belly inside a wedding gown.
Her twin sister—eyebrows gorgeous as a painting
on a folding screen.
Then the first and second wives of my grandfather,
who'd been in big trouble for having an affair
with the wife of a doctor of Asian medicine.

My old family photos...

All the women, standing in good spirits
on a snowy day before I was born,
celebrating moving into a newly-built house.
They called a photographer from the town
to take this family photograph—
The women, dressed *a la mode*, all smile.

This strangely beautiful
old family photograph,
taken before I was even born.

A Room Where I Cry Alone

I remodeled my new place before moving in,
converting a cozy room next to the kitchen
into a place for crying alone.
Having a room for sobbing,
I'm already a poet, radiant
and with a bright future,
a crane secretly weaving silk,
spinning the whirring wheel all night.
Or a snail-damsel who turns human only when alone.
At dawn, if I were asked to write my biography,
I'd write: My tears are my hometown,
my alma mater, my wounds.

A Speedboat at 'Night

Awakened by insomnia at one a.m.,
I drag, push my body
into the hazy mirror.
A gray hair dashes with bravado across my forehead,
like a speedboat cutting across the water
in the midst of a dark river.
Oh, why did I let this crazy woman drag me
into the land of the tender elderly,
to the land of unknown mysteries?
With all my strength, I pluck the damned hair out.
Come out!
How dare you appear so soon,
dispiriting me.
If I pluck all my gray hairs out,
I may end up bald.

Wagging My Tail

My little secret is the tail on my rear end.
If I confessed, people would say
I'm quite good at metaphor.
It would be embarrassing to show them the real McCoy,
so they'd better take me at my word.

At last, I have a tail instead of wings,
and I kind of like having one.
Sometimes I touch it, just for fun.
Wings can be dangerous,
but a tail, if well wagged, enhances.

I like the word *tail*.
As you move your lips to say it,
you feel its subtle nuance.
It holds the relief of being the last, the end,
the touch of the essence of things.
It looks like a soldier's secret scar.
No, it looks like a rather cute fox.
If I wag my tail, will my love hold on to it
and beg me not to leave?

Oh, I have something even Venus doesn't have.
Shall I enchant you by wagging it now?

Cold Rice

Alone, I rise from my sick bed
to eat cold, leftover rice.
so cold it hurts my sore throat.
So many kitchen appliances—
I could warm it up
with just the push of a button.
I don't have to eat it cold, but I'm trying,
reminiscing about the woman who cooked
hot rice for her family but always ate cold rice alone
from a cracked bowl, and sucked someone else's
radish stems and fish bones.
Yet she emitted love.
I feel an irresistable yearning for her hands,
and the clattering noises of dishes being washed
late at night.

Today, I rise from my sick bed
and eat cold, leftover rice.
God can't be present in every home,
so he sends a mother to each one.
I see her in the cold rice.
Today, I've become cold rice.

Missing the Goblins

Inside the terra cotta outhouse
roughly built in the bamboo grove
lived frightening, horned goblins,
even during the day.

When nature called
mother accompanied her small child,
holding tight to a lantern with both hands.
While she kept guard,
I lifted my skirt and sat on the seat.
I heard birds gossiping in the grove
and saw countless bright stars giggling away.
When mother gently wiped my porcelain skin
with a sagebrush leaf,
its fragrance spread everywhere,
making the goblins shiver and shake.

When the little princess
visited the terra cotta palace
built in the bamboo grove,
whether two or three times a day,
this beautiful ritual took place.

Lies

Suppose I meet my old flame again
in a pub somewhere in the south of Seoul
and confess in a tremulous voice,
"I've never forgotten you."
Would that true?
We'd both believe it's a lie—
yet, its not completely untrue.
While we share a few drinks
our past lives dissolve like lies
or like truth.
When we recognize the transcience
of the waves of words washed away—
who are we then?
Poets, the pair of us.

Memories

I still don't know why
I wasn't young even when I was young.
Things frequently blurred.
Lost in the lonely evening darkness,
I panted like a horse with a heavy load.
I knew only the burdens of life.
Although each day began with music
and I spent entire days hunting,
I couldn't find the boar I pursued.
Perhaps my mother wasn't my mother.
I didn't know she'd given me
an inscrutable black seed
in addition to life itself.
I still don't know why
I burned with agony when I was young.
I roamed the city tossing them off
like so many unwanted stones—
those fresh, blue moments of my youth.

Confessions of a Hand

Gazing at our hands
we realize they didn't always seize at desires.
Strolling the narrow path of bygone memories
we sense that they more often let things pass.
Even letting our first love go,
we nonchalantly waved our hands, like flags.
Those who crouch inside all day
like wounded animals in the dark
know the truth.
All desire lost, standing precariously
on a precipitious cliff,
their steps were like the ticking of a clock.

As we gaze at our hands
in a torrential bombardment
by the latest fashionable tragedy,
by happiness as a cheap hamburger,
as we gaze at our hands,
unable to get up and walk,
like animals buried alive,
we know that the narrow path
of bygone memories
suddenly—in reminiscence—
winds its way back to us.

Green Onions

I cut their roots off with a big kitchen knife.
I scream inside as I cut off the roots
that clenced the soil until the end.

Why can't marriage be like a bird?
Why is it tenacious and persistent, like roots?
Living like a feather blowing freely around—
is that something to fear
or to be so uneasy about?
Must we always celebrate settling down?
Why should we reproduce and multiply, like cows?
Why should we always be paired?
When will my dark hair turn white, like onion roots?

Today, I sliced off the green onions' roots
using the biggest and sharpest knife I own.
Then I chopped those green onions
and threw them in the boiling stew.

Why We Must Love

We must love each other
because we share the earth's water,
we share the vegetation of the earth.
Under the same sun and moon,
we all wrinkle and grow old.
And we should love each other
because we all cry while throwing time's stones
into the rivers of the earth.
We tumble in the wind
without knowing one another.
Like falling leaves or scuttling beetles,
we are all separated and dispersed.

The Drunken Poet

In a word, we have a "relationship."
We've traveled together this far.
Now, just hearing his voice on the telelpone
I know how many cups of *soju* he's drunk.
Even in those days when the dictator
forced us to wear uniforms
and we looked like the poplar trees
that line the banks of the Han,
we wrote poems together, swaying in strong winds.
Dauntless, we saw our future in poetry.
In youth, we suffered endless psychic trauma,
but who cared? We still had poetry.

Time, that dictator, dragged us this far.
We still write poems in the sand,
shake leaves despite injuring their roots.
Drunk, he utters casually, gazing at me,
"I want to do it with you just once before I die."
We've come this far together.
What shall I do?
Should I tell him, before it's too late,
"I want to do it with you, too,"?
Would he be scared and run away?
But who cares?
We've already lost our way.

Landscape With Funeral Lantern

We hurriedly hung the funeral lantern.
People began to arrive
but no one cried,
because Mother lived until eighty,
a long life. I pretended to cry
because she'd been bedridden for so long.
Now Mother was truly dead.
My mother, those tears.
She was dead.
Something astonishing happened that evening:
I began to feel hungry!
Although Mother was gone forever,
my stomach cried out for food.
Someone brought me something to eat,
and as I reluctantly ate, pretending I had no appetite,
my hometown relatives rushed in.
They bowed a moment before Mother's portrait
and for the first time in decades, held my hands.
They consoled me, saying,
"Oh, aren't you her youngest child? You look so old."
With no hesitation, they threw me into the pit
with a final precision shot:
"I barely recognized her.
She looks just like her mom."

Song for Soldiers

Perhaps you don't know this,
but every woman in this land
once fell in love with a soldier.
All this land's young men
once went in uniform to the DMZ,
bearing arms against their brothers in the North,
learning life's intense yearning and bittersweet agony.
Every woman in this land
wrote consoling letters to soldiers when young,
went to visit them at army camps when they grew up.
But love does not always ripen.
Often, in the passing years, paths diverged.
When, years later, a woman encounters
her old flame—dressed in a business suit
and in the sunset of his life—shy and embarrassed,
she silently cries at the realization
that a barrier rustier than the DMZ blocks the path of life.
Perhaps you don't know this,
but every woman in this land
once fell in love with a soldier.

Part III

Night of the Pomegranate

I sink my teeth into your heart.
Your fragrant red blood flows through my teeth.

I want to look in the mirror
and see a woman eating her lover's heart.
No matter how much she eats, still hungry,
like a witch, she devours his head.
Oh, my love.
Little by little, she devours his words.
Waking in the middle of the night, she eats you.

Forgive Me, Daughter

Forgive me, daughter,
I have to say this today:
Screaming in fury
at the disgraceful colonization
of our homeland by our enemy,
my throat trembles with tears.
I don't know what "nation" or "people" mean,
but I don't believe they refer only to men.
The reason I kneel and cry before you today,
the reason I apologize,
dragging out my indifference and forgetfulness again,
is because I depise my ignorance and self-righteousness
more than I hate those Japanese soldiers
who made you a trophy, stole your integrity and dignity.
I'm ashamed of the fathers and brothers of this land
who survived by selling women like Simchong and Hongdo
while idling their time away flirting with *kisaeng*,
driving women to the red light district. Daughter,
we saw you helplessly being dragged to the warfront
to serve as a comfort woman in the ruthless
sex slave system of the Japanese.
I kneel before you today and sincerely apologize
not on behalf of "nation" or "people,"
not for the mental wounds and shame
inflicted on your psyches bys men,
but on behalf of the dignity and integrity
being nothing but a trophy stole from you.

I'm so sorry, daughter.
I truly am.

Wedding Train

Every journey has a destination,
except this one.
If I want to alight from this train
before death do us part,
I'll have to cut off the leg
that's chained to his.

Oh, marriage is important,
but not as important as life.
If marriage places me in jeopardy,
I'd rather sever it from my life.

Occasionally, someone leaps from the train,
bravely cutting off a leg.
Standing on just one leg,
he hears the other leg calling
from the the train.
In search of that missing leg,
she catches another train.

Looking out the window
I often hesitate—
"Shall I get off at the next station?"
Grabbing the children's hands,
I stare at the heavy bundles on the rack.
Meanwhile the train goes through twilight
and into a long tunnel.

Passengers constantly get on board
this comfortable train with no destination.

Could There Be Trees on that Mountain?

Could there be trees on that mountain,
with green hair streaming in the wind?
Could it be a young man, a thousand years old?
When the moon rises above his brow,
will there be animals offering prayers
while sitting on wounded knees?
As new babies are born each season,
are there women who change their soft diapers
before a transparent mirror that changes hourly?
As I have thunder and lightning inside me,
a rock melting secretly, hiding its forehead in fog,
are there thunder and lightning in that mountain?
Does someone exhale rough breath, take an arduous step
right this moment toward a higher peak
and staggering because of vertigo,
wonder whether to go up or down?

Is there someone on the hillside suffering like me?

Waiting for a Hawk

Gazing at the pouring rain,
all I could think of was an umbrella
and a cozy, sheltering abode,
or writing a poem, using words
my mother taught me
and imagining the rainbow it would hold.

But today, in the fierce rain
following such long drought,
I see a strong young man
letting emerald streams gush forth,
allowing patches of blue radishes to grow.

I see a hawk ruffling its feathers to soar into the sky,
a hawk that transforms itself into thunder—
a revolutionary who commands the crowd
with his thundering voice,
sweeping everything on earth away.

Melancholy

Winter fog along an endless tunnel.
The serene insanity of an afternoon in middle-age.
I walk into grayness, seeing not a single light.
My purse holds a bunch of keys,
but I don't want a single one.
God may have no monopoly on miracles.
I've lived them every day of my life.
But now, looking back on those days, I see
rocking chairs that used to endlessly squeak
sitting silently on an empty stage.

Rhapsody for the Throat

Embracing your throat
is like embracing a marble pillar
in a temple of the gods.
I want to make red flowers bloom
in our very own *sanctum sanctorum*.

Like a cricket in the forest
I want to cry all night
as desolate winds caress my hair.

I want to take aim at your throat.
Like a vampire in a desolate castle,
I want to sink my fangs in passionately
and suck out your rolling-thunder breath.
I want to possess you tonight.

Camellia

Nowhere to go now.
Drinking brandy laced with laudanum,
love leaps from a steep cliff.
This most glamorous flower
is just another name
for the most glamorous death.

With no place left to go,
drinking brandy laced with laudanum,
love jumps off a cliff at the end of a thousand roads.
This dazzling flower
is just another name
for the most eloquent death.

Cutting Hair

In the village in the valley
where salamanders, goats
and poor, ragged children grow
like red-ribboned blooms,
on the day I see a saintly old man
with a long beard and scissors,
I'll cover my shoulders
with newspaper
and have him cut my long hair.

The day I yearn for nothing,
the day I'm no longer sad,
I'll stop complaining
like a divorced daughter
who's returned to her family home.
I'll cut off the thousand tributaries
of that dark river
with the soft sound of melting snow.

Skirt

Men instinctively know
there's something special there.
There's surely something special beneath a skirt.
It swirls like a fierce tornado,
hides the waxing and waning moon,
the temple between two pale pillars.
Maybe God lives there.
Men, eternal tourists, loiter
near that forbidden sanctuary
hoping to to find the secret of life.
If God's not there, then maybe one of his kin.
That's why men, desperate to continue
their bloodline, breed their successors there.
Perhaps it obscures a hidden sea
with an amazingly beautiful tideland
where clams dream.
Is it a cave—
a cave where, once entered,
you're doomed to die?
The surprising thing is,
it's more powerful when removed.

Caterpillar Dream

Have you ever dreamed of being a caterpillar?
I'd rather be a baby caterpillar than a bookworm.
A bookworm, unable to build a home,
wriggles and gnaws at dark words,
but a caterpillar tries to reach the sky,
rowing on a green leaf raft
even though swinging from a slender twig.
Not a greedy, devouring money worm
nor a hungry worm consuming all the fruit
and leaving holes in every single leaf.

Have you ever dreamed of being a caterpillar?
I want to be a baby caterpillar
living in the heart of my lover,
shining like a tiny twinkling star.

Woman Who Lives in the Green Tree

Roaming the field in spring rain,
I realize that a woman lives in the soil.
Who else could care with such devotion
for the burgeoning tufts of grass and the flock of birds?
Strolling the field in spring rain,
I want to become a green child
whom the woman in the soil raises and tends.
Or I want to raise children, too,
fresh as green grass and agile as a flock of birds.
I want at least one child always by my side,
rubbing our cheeks together,
walking the field in spring rain.
Suddenly I realize a woman dwells in that tree,
her green hands clasped in constant prayer.

To My Sweetheart

Sweetheart, when summer comes
bring me a pair of red-handled scissors
to cut wayward branches, neatly
trimming my futile desires.
When branches pile high on the ground,
use them to build a birdhouse in the air.
I'll raise a bird
that sways each time the wind blows
and sings when it hatches its eggs.

Mask

The word "truth" has often made me cry,
but today I also like the word "hypocrisy,"
the merry mask that says, "I still love you."
Without it, I would have fallen, bleeding.
Yes, it's saved so many families,
so many deteriorating friendships,
so many men from criminal intent.

The word "truth" has often made me cry,
but today I realize that
it's not the crystal clear "truth"
but back alley hypocrisy
that sustains us—
like the big tree that shades us,
like we, who rest in its shade.

A Tomb in the Air

His tomb is in the air—
the man who hanged himself
from a tree at the entrance to the village
right after the war, when I was seven years old.

When serenity fell over the village
in the gorgeous twilight,
he was floating in air, like a cloud.
Who was he—
this man who limped from alley to alley
driven by village urchins throwing stones?
This man who closed his eyes in agony,
saying he'd seen something terrible:
a man killing another man.
This man who spit on the road
and limped around town,
who was one day lifted into the air.

When it's overcast, I still feel a soft cloud
lingering on my shoulders.

Sophia

Is it, as the poet said, better
to be homesick than to remain
in the town of your youth?
No, I'd choose to live in you
rather than in nostalgia.
People like poems about
tomorrow and yesterday,
but that's not my choice today.
I want to go to Sophia
to feel the fire,
to set myself aflame.
Someone once told me
to beware of fire;
it's not a necessity of life.
They said life is stagnant,
doesn't burn like a torch.
Is that why my songs are dangerous,
why birds choose to live in my heart?
I don't know where Sophia is,
but I want to go there today—
not tomorrow, not yesterday.
I want to go there today.
I want you, not nostaglia.
I want to live in you.

The Rose

Is a poet beautiful,
an existence who gives life
to the roses that bloom upon time?
Does she have a life or only words?
In her prison, she sees only a hand
writing a poem as she sits alone.
Blind as an owl,
her eyes open to poetry.
For her reality is always a curse,
love is always a parting.
From her solitary cell, she sets words free
to fall in love with one another, lay a golden egg.
Poetry, child not of silence
but of words—
love never spoken
blooms in her poems
like a fresh rose.

For the Poet

She wrote many poems
before she died.
Only the poems remain.
The many people who read them
come to know her mistakes and human flaws,
but only by her poetry
may she be reproached.
Her exquisite words and moving lines
pose constant questions about her life.
Some are blinded by the jewels she left behind;
others, driven crazy by her flowering soul-search,
cast doubts, call it brilliant fabrication
and try to knock it down by casting stones.
Yet, this brings her poetry more vigorously to life.
It becomes blood red, ruby red,
a warm, unencumbered heart.
Many who read her poems,
left passionate and breathless,
berate the poet
and suffer her torment.

Part IV

His Last Bed

What is this? Is this how it ends?
Sometimes my life has been empty,
sometimes it's been full,
but reduced to nothing more than an old animal?
Words I loved so long already extinguished beyond hope.
This can't be the end. It should work the other way around.
I'd rather be born an old animal,
grow into a lucid, glamorous adult,
and end my life as a lovely child—
or maybe as an egg
returned to my mother's womb
or to the entire earth.
Did God create humans?
Did he make this pathetic body?
Senility rather than a light mind,
a rag rather than bones.
Is this how God's work ends?
After overcoming pain, injury
and pricking thorns,
what is this? Is this how it ends?

With My Camera

I passed the zelkova, crossed the stone bridge,
and there was my old hometown,
but no home was waiting for me.
My old friend Choonsun, the tennis player, was dead.
My crippled friend Hobum was long gone too.
The cousins who ran my uncle's mill had dispersed.
No more rabbit hunting or the sound of a guitar.
After a photographer from Gwangju came to take pictures
of the old people for their encroaching funerals,
young widows suddenly gave birth.
Among them was a widow with yellow, waxy eyes—
Widow Mole—who ate poison mushrooms and died.
Her pug-nosed children were all gone too.
My friends Youngtae and Samsik,
who were strong enough to carry heavy bundles of rice,
are buried in the reedy graveyard on the far hill.
Only a rock covered with pumpkin blossoms greeted me.
An *ondol* chimney beneath a low hanging roof
remained silent, even though I shook it.
Someone's black dog began to bark at me.
I was a stranger in my own hometown.
My camera photographed only absence and Nirvana.
I couldn't find my home in my own hometown.
I felt like I wasn't even real.

Where Is My Home?

My mother's womb, my first home,
turned to dust in the cemetery of Ilsan Park.
The home on Wonhyoro Street in Seoul
where I left childhood behind
is a clinic for plastic surgery now.
The Mapo home where I spent my teen years
listening to the government's propaganda
is filled with municipal offices,
and gorgeous Balm Island is now gone.
Near the Blue House, Jimnyung Girls' High School,
my alma mater, is a government building, too.
The home where I spent my college years
in Sangdo-dong has become a cheap hotel.
Frogs once croaked near my newlywed home in Kui-dong.
Now, a convenience store stands there.
Today, I'm driven from the white villa
near Youngdong Bridge,
and looking for a place to rent.

Gazing at the specter of a white villa demolished for a development
which advertises that "Ownership gives you pride,"
I imagine a magic castle emerging in its place.
Where can I place all my memories,
the vestiges of what remains as only tears?
Memories are giving me this headache.
I drag my memories—love, sorrow, burdens—
along like a child, by the hand.
I feel like the last survivor of this era
about to be dragged to a museum in a desolate place.
I can't find myself anywhere.
Can this be my native land?

Grinding Coffee Beans

I still love useless things—
songs and yearnings,
wounds and raindrops,
and I love autumn, Mother.
I still write poems
while drinking more coffee
than I eat regular meals.
I fall asleep embracing books
and love wandering more than my job.
I still love pine trees
standing in strong winds,
lonely stars and deserts,
wild storms.

I know I could make money on war or human waste.
Some of my friends have already left for the city
where they'll grope for money in the urban wasteland
while yearning for a home
where good-natured people
dressed in white, like saints,
though unable to read a single line
of the Bible or Buddhist scripture,
peacefully farm the land.
Mother, I still plow dry earth.

Landscape with Mad Birds

Spring has come, but no one's noticed.
This spring of 2003,
no blossoms, no green leaves.
Only fireworks that bloom like flowers.
Black birds, flying in a column,
dive toward the heart of a desert city.
These new migratory birds
called "missiles"
dash toward crying children.
Gazing at them, women's eyes are blank.

The spring of 2003— trick of mad birds, dark flames.
People watching the news at dinnertime, faces grim,
anxiously telephone friends and relatives.
But they soon brush off their sense of guilt,
turn the TV off and forget about the war.

The surrealistic spring of 2003 came and went,
and nobody noticed anything.

Apartment Cave

Our apartment building has been under repair since yesterday.
It's like a dinosaur, with no water, power outtages,
the elevator motionless, like a fossilized vertebrae.
The reisidents are like cavemen now.
As night approaches, hungry, they take bloody
meat from the dark refrigerator
and begin to eat,
The toilet spilled over, spreading manure-like stench.
Like a woman possesed, I scuffle along the wall in the dark
to fiddle with the dead switch. I twist the faucet handle
and reach out, upside down, with my mouth.

Our building's been under repair since yesterday.
In a single day, we've turned into
primitive savages, barbaric animals,
hopelessly trapped in our cave.

Although I Love the Sky

Although I love the sky,
I think it rules over me too much.
When it blinds me with bright sun,
when it rains or snows,
it disrupts my life.
With my low roof and flimsy clothing,
I can't evade it's watchful gaze.
All scars appear pale blue,
yearning for the color of the sky.
Today, as I write this poem
in my quiet room,
the sky is clear.
Is that because the sky loves me, too?

Water Lilies

What words are adequate
for the water lilies' new blooms?
It would be disgraceful
for a poet to pass these dazzling flowers
without a word.
But unable to reach them
or touch them with my lips,
I can only let my dazzling smile,
like a blossom, unfold
until my dewy eyes' translucent drops
make their blue sky tremble.

'Balloon

Play with me,
float me high,
fill me with hot air.
Blow me up a little more,
my soft skin grows taut.
Fumble with me, pop me.
No, touch me tenderly.
I might burst at any moment.
My entire body is as vulnerable
as an icy road
exposed to the sharp
slings and arrows of time.
No need for a key to open me,
just throw me to the wind.
No, kill me with excitement.

A Call From Seoul

A telephone call from Seoul
screams in the middle of the night:

What I'm living for eludes me.
Here, people make millions overnight
from real estate investments.
Everyday the traffic is so congested,
the air so filthy I can barely breathe.
Television is ever more disgusting
but bored, I fix it in my gaze.
In a city teeming with liars and hypocrites,
even poets are sometimes disingenuous
and follow their leaders in droves.
They use drunkeness as symbolic ornament,
but it's merely a twinge of conscience or an alibi.
Even members of the audience climb onstage,
stampeding in their blind desire for fame,
their yearning for mundane success.
Many have found fame and been awarded,
but I've seldom enthusiastically clapped.
Seoul rolls along now like a rickety bus
that will explode the minute it brakes.
Happiness is difficult to find.

Why does he think happiness always comes from pain?
Why does he mistake it for misery and defeat?

When I hung up, I wanted to return to Seoul right away.
If his pain-filled happiness
and my lonely happiness could wed,
and gave birth to something new,
would I be a real poet then?

Longing for Seoul's madness and rush,
I stayed up all night packing my bags.

To the Sand of the World

You, sand of the world, arise
and block the barrels of all guns
until handfuls of sand become rock.
Flow for a thousand days
like the endless river
of motherly anxiety and care,
flow toward green mountains
like the bloodline of life,
bloom like flowers, then fall like the palaces
that burn beneath desert sands.
Oh, last night's restless dreams!
Oh, dreams that turn, at last, to sand!
Arise in a storm and block the barrels of all guns.
Obscure the fearful road to weaponry.
Stop the tanks rolling toward the screams.
Sand of the North, sand of the South!
Make clear the bloodshot eyes of brothers
who've stared at one another for fifty years.
You, sand of the world, turn, at last, to rock.

Who Are You?

An aerodynamic body built for supersonic speed.
no man has ever loved me
or been as faithful to me as you.
You're never jealous or restless.
While I mingle with others
you wait for me, calmly, where you were left.
Perhaps I'd better marry you
so I can transport my 130 pound body
with your 3500 pound hulk.

Wherever we go, streets are clogged like veins.
Cud-de-sacs and labyrinths are everywhere.
People blindly love the way you rush forward,
like the unknown monsters in primordial woods.
You live with us. You're found everywhere.
Who are you?
Where are you from?

Scandal Cat

As I was leafing through the morning paper,
from its pages, a black cat leaped.
I quickly turned on the TV
and his name was floating in mud
like a pig afloat in a flood.
Handcuffs on his wrists flashed, silver,
as he covered his face in shame.
His crime could easily be seen.
He built a house of sand,
taking secret bribes in the dark
like a cat sneakily licking rice cakes
or jumping on an antique chair.
I remember this cat's spring days.
He's posed, on a village poster,
holding in his arms a child,
bright smile on his innocent face.
I saw him wearing a white armband
while picking up trash and planting
seedlings along the road.
That scene, so real, was frightening,
like some sort of a strange horror film.
I closed that cat into the newspaper
and threw it in the trash can near my house.
There was no possibility of recycling.
The stench was too intense.

Love from the Ground

The 350-year-old mummy of a child, wrapped in silk, was exhumed
from the Yun family graveyard in Kyunggi Province, South Korea.

Son, how could I bury you beneath the ground?
Your crystal-clear eyes,
your pearly teeth shining in morning sun.
How could I bury my precious treasure
beneath the frozen earth?
My lovely seven-year-old son, his page already turned?
The sky is falling
The entire world grows cold.
I spread your father's silk coat over you
and cover you with my jacket, which is interwoven
with excruciating pain that even the sickness
that killed you couldn't penetrate.
When your mother and father watched black dirt
tumble down the steep sides of your grave,
the sun and the moon disappeared.
How could time destroy you?

If You Have a Broom

If you have a broom in your hands
come into my heart.
Sweep out the useless leaves,
take away the flower vase
and the dust-covered chair.
As you sit, by habit, in the living room,
send your breath into the clock
that only runs backward, to memories,
so that it will bring forth a new day.
If you have a broom in your hands,
sweep the solitary shadows from my back.
Make a path for dazzling new beams.

Birthday

A young whale lived inside of me,
a blue whale, when I was just twenty years old.
When I was thirty and a cello,
I'd spread my legs a bit while sitting on a chair
and scratch my back like a contented man,
sweaty and smelling like stale tobacco smoke.
When I was forty, I pinned a black rose
to my black dress and listened to a requiem.
Like a Western woman who's over-the-hill,
I was choked, without reason, with tears.
When I'm fifty, I'll be unbearably light—
with nothing left to grab.
Even love will be light as a breeze,
half-empty but still fulfilling.

What will my fiftieth birthday be like?
Praying costs nothing and might be heard.
Shall I, piteously, pray?

What We Cannot Own

The most beautiful thing isn't meant to be touched—
a dazzling smile blooming
among flowers and trees.

The most precious things aren't meant to be owned–
calendar photos of gorgeous girls,
the memory of fine poetic words.

The loveliest thing isn't meant to be hidden—
the light that shines in lovers' eyes
as they gaze at one another.

A Long Journey

I found God in these shoes.
It was such a long journey,
and no road was familiar to me;
I just put on these shoes and walked.

On the first day, I learned to walk
with shoes between me and the earth.
I staggered step by step
until I found myself here.

How light are the shoes birds wear?
What sort grace river and wind?

These shoes I wear now,
not wise nor firm, unlike the roots of trees,
shall I take them off?

Should I sit by the river
and learn the freedom of the stream?

Life is but a steep set of stairs
that refuses to touch the sky.

Coming to this faraway place,
I utter, in awe, God's name.

In shoes that long to walk the earth
is where my God resides.

Part V

Morning Dew

What profound meditations last night
brought forth, translucent on a blade
of grass, this morning dew?
Was it agony? A bit of life,
starlight, sorrow's flesh and bones?
Who could give birth to this diamond?
Is pain, like morning dew, soft and cold?

Love is
a brief climax, a brief and precious drop
even the sound of breathing cannot penetrate.
After a long journey through the night,
what message does this
morning dew form on leaves
that precariously hold this transparent
and transient moment?

Putting on Makeup

Painting my lips scarlet,
I see in the mirror a vain princess, all made up—
my small face an array of international cities,
a theater where fictitious dramas
staged by cosmetic illusionists converge,
a small territory where lavish flags wave.

Sexy brown is the color *a la mode* this fall.
Rouging my cheeks, as Chanel instructs,
adhering to the myth of glamour,
I realize the conspiracy is almost complete.
Occasionally frightened at my mind's enslavement,
I'm once again bewitched by cloying perfume,
an apparition painted in soft tones,
and my sporadic protests are weak.

To stop time's winged chariot,
need I be adorned in such sad fragrance?
With Estee Lauder eyeliner, I carefully
draw a dark border around my eyes
and dab a drop of Christian Dior behind my ears.
The colonized *femme élégante* ready to *sortie!*
She makes her entrance slowly, like a tragic heroine.

His Wife

The night of the theater's fireworks display,
I saw his wife.
Around her neck, she wore a slender chain
adorned with tiny, almost invisible gems.
Perhaps it was his birthday gift to her,
or commemorates their first child's birth.
Maybe it's a quarrel's make-up gift,
or a reward for the care she gave his mother,
well now after being bedridden for so many years.

Like evening stars embroidered
on sea urchins on the shore,
I notice on her the delicate,
yet tenacious,
traces he's left behind,
patterns woven into her with the lapse of time
which no outsider can possibly infiltrate.

But I'm just a stranger passing by
from a remote place.
What's the harm in imagining us
having an unexpected, romantic affair?
The moment I saw her
I knew we'd inevitably
be reduced to melodrama
or a brief and hopeless fling.
Quietly standing behind him,
probably buying his suits,
she's inconspicious as unnoticed cornerstones.
But that night, among the crowd,
I couldn't take my eyes off of her.

A Valley

In the forest of gray apartment buildings,
a valley has just been opened up.
Entering the urban cornucopia
inside this huge mart,
everyone is greeted by a shoping cart.
People follow their carts like sheep
as they lead them past the tempting shops
and toward the final exit.
They flock together like migratory birds,
and pile mounds of groceries in their carts.
Deceived by the word "credit,"
they toss more and more into the carts.
They won't have to pay now anyway.
After meandering through the aisles,
they arrive at the check-out counter
where they look like happy consumers.
Standing in line, they proudly sign
their credit card slips, happy to be
in this procession.
They rush everyday to the valley,
like migratory birds flocking toward a net.

To a Spider

Spider, I am well aware
of how desperately you embrace
empty space, of your immense vanity.

In last night's flashing thunderstorm,
the howling of thousands of wolves.
This morning in the giant trees, green leaves.

In that wonderland—
to hang a few drops of glistening tears,
to engrave a dazling rainbow on space.

Oh, what a poet!
What resplendent silk threads you weave!
How you dip your pen in the hot blood of your heart!

Daffodil

Nobody knows that she who floats
on air today like a feather's tender soul
sat in meditation, on the roadside,
covered in dust last spring.
While trees straightened their green spines,
and seaweed built castles under the sea,
she lamented, her face near the ground,
listening to the dead beneath the earth,
Like mountain hermits who've left home
to become, akin to a Buddha, light
when they reach a certain age,
she arose one late spring day,
a charming smile on her face,
and left the other flowers behind.
When she ascended, knees bent,
her place on earth was left clean—
only scattered earth on the newly filled grave.
Upon the grass, she left no trace.

Appreciating My Hometown

I'm grateful to my hometown.

With all those trees,
it taught me green.
With all those birds,
it made me sing.
With all that rain,
it made me cry the tears
that enrich all lives.

I'm grateful to my hometown.

With all those rivers,
it showed me how time flows.
With all those butterflies,
it made me miss my loved ones
when they went away.
And with all those roads,
it made me a poet.

When a Jewel on Your Finger Glitters

When you read this poem,
you may forget the poet's tears.
When a jewel on your finger glitters,
you may forget the dark, dry skin
and the torn fingernails caked with mud
of the woman who wears ragged clothing
as she pans with a shabby basket for gold.

Who's been to the realm of profound silence
to write poems, excavate tears?
How sad their confessions,
how loud the thunder's roar.
Why the jewel glitters brightly,
you don't need to know.

When a lovely fragrance fills the wind,
when a gorgeous poem fills the mind,
when a jewel on a finger glitters,
you forget the bloodied poet's tears.

When I Wish I Were a Donkey

Sometimes I wish I were a donkey.
Sometimes I want to endlessly roam
even if it's not a moonlit night.
When the whirlwind of a sandstorm
whips my skin, I wish
I could blink like a donkey,
and stamp my feet.

Why did our ancestors so long ago
build this road winding rather than straight?
I carry sorrow and pleasure
in my every nook and cranny,
savoring life a little at a time.
I want to be part of a caravan
always on the move.

Feeling on my back
your precious weight,
I want to believe
it's a holy book.

Each time I trip on a protruding stone,
I want to stamp on the ground
to the beat of my throbbing heart.

Tale of a Home

Women are born
with a home of their own,
so they don't need one on earth.
Only men need homes in this world.
Behold! Men bleed all through their lives,
carrying cement or bricks on their backs
to build a home—
eternal construction workers,
they piously wear a touch of eternal grief.
They often bear their lot by swearing,
and strew liquor bottles around the site
as they conspire to justify an equal distribution of wealth.
Those men we love spend their lives on the battlefield
building a barracks that will soon to be blown away.
They say men often return to their home,
their birthplace, to die.
History is full of inscrutable mysteries:
imagine being born with a home in your own body.

No wonder women
are constantly persecuted
and invaded.

Song of Arrows

When I say this,
I always cry a bit.

In your life you'll use more words
than you'll use fire, water, or money,
so gather your words and use them well

People compare words not to swords
but to arrows, for like arrows,
words, once used, don't return.

In a thick woods of pointed arrows
there's a heart pierced by words
that spread poison or fire.

When I fall in love with fresh new words,
it's like the first chapter of a new-found holy book,
and I cry a little, my lips tremulous.

I'll use more words
than I'll use fire, water or money,
for words are the most precious things I own.

When I say this,
I always cry a bit.

The Boy

The taxi I barely caught at the terminal was dirty and old.
The driver, upset for some reason, didn't begin to pull away
until I uttered again, "Samsung-dong!"
Then he violently tossed his cigarette butt out the window,
stomped on the accelerator like mad, and began to swear.
Former owner of a seafood restaurant in Samsung-dong,
he went bankrupt when the rent was doubled one day.
Now my life was in this bullet-fast driver's hands
until I reached my destination.
Detecting a familiar accent in his dialect,
I asked if he might be from my hometown.
He retorted that he'd once dated a girl from there.
While wondering if this would make a satire or a lyrical poem,
I suddenly saw him as a romantic boy
who, one summer suffered unrequited love
for a girl from Seoul too glamourous
for a shabby country boy, too far beyond his reach.
Then one autumn day, her letter arrived.
Thrilled, but overwhelmed, he couldn't open it,
so one of his friends snatched it away and threw it in the river.
Now, while driving through the city's rivers of light at night,
in his mind, he still sees that boy, silently sobbing,
hopelessly watching the torrent swallow his letter up.
I arrrived safely in Sansung-dong at last and got out,
but the boy in that taxi refused to fade away.

Notes on the Poems

Page 17: In a Korean folk tale, Gyunwoo, a cow herder, and Jiknyo, a spinster, break the rule of forbidden love and as a punishment are only allowed to see each other on July 7 each year on a bridge in the Milky Way. If it rains on that day, which is very likely, Koreans believe it is the couple weeping with joy.

Page 19: "Moon" is the poet's name. In Korean, moon also reads door.

Page 21: In Korean legend, Nankrang (108 B.C.–313 A.D.) was an ancient state located on the Korean Peninsula. Nankrang was protected by a magic drum that automatically sounded whenever a foreign country was about to invade. In 28 A.D., Prince Hodong of Goguryo was sent by his father to infiltrate Nankrang and destroy the drum so they could attack without advance warning. Hodong met and fell in love with with the princess of Nankrang. She returned his love, and to help him, she cut the skin off of the war drum. She was killed by her father as retribution for her treasonable act, and Hodong mourned while holding her lifeless body. This great Korean love story was made into the film *Prince Hodong* in 1962.

Page 22: *The Story of Simchong* is a well-known classic of Korean literature. Siimchong was a filial daughter who was born to a poor family. As her mother died in childbirth and her father was blind, she had to support her father. One day her father, without thinking, pledged to offer three hundred bushels of rice to his Buddhist temple so that he could regain his sight.

It just so happened that Chinese merchants were looking for a maiden to be sacrificed to appease the Dragon King of the East Sea, who freuently sent storms to sink ships. Simchong offered herself in exchange for the three hundred bushels of rice for her father. When a great storm hit the ship, Simchong leapt overboard into the sea and the violent tempet became calm once again. As Simchong descended in the water, she was warmly received by the Dragon King, who took her as his queen. Once married, Simchong grew homesick and dearly missed her father so much that she threw a party for blind men, hoping her father might come. He did, and she was finally reunited with her father, who opened his eyes in surprise.

Page 28: Ingak Temple is located in Gooneui, Byeongsang Province in South Korea. It is where the famous Buddhist monk Ilyon (1206–1289) wrote *Samguk Yusa (Memorabilia of the Three Kingdoms.)*

Page 54: Every Wednesday afternoon, former Korean comfort women, dressed in white, gather in front of the Japanese embassy in Seoul to demand an apology from the Japanese government. *Kisaeng* are similar to Japanese geisha.

Page 56: Hongdo is the female protagonist of *Don't Cry, Hongo!* by playwright Im Sun-gyu, who wrote this work in the mid-twentieth century. To support her brother, who is in college, Hongdo becomes a *kisaeng*. Thanks to her sacrifice, her brother eventually becomes a prosecutor. But her dark past becomes a fatal flaw when she gets married. She is treated badly by her in-laws and deserted by her husband, simply because she was once a *kisaeng*. Persecuted by her mean in-laws, she accidentally kills one of them. Ironically, Hongdo is prosecuted by her own brother. This sad story has been made into a pop song which has been enormously popular in Korea.

Page 59: This poem references the book *Camille,* in which the beautiful heroine dies a tragic death. Laudanum is reddish colored tincture of opium used for medicinal purposes.

Page 70: Sophia is the Greek word for "wisdom." It refers in the poem to an idealistic place like El Dorado.

Page 76 : A zelkova is a deciduous tree native to Asia and southern Europe.
Ondol is a heating system that conducts the flue gases of a fire located below the ground level of the house under the floor of a living space. A short chimney to provide the draft for the system rises from the ground on the side of the house.
In a Korean funeral, a photograph of the deceased is placed on the closed coffin.

Page 77: Ilsan is a suburb located north of Seoul. Balm Island is a small island located in the heart of Seoul in the middle of the River Han. The Blue House is the official rsidence of the President of the Republic of Korea. It is located in downtown Seoul. Sangdo-dong and Kui-dong are two districts in Seoul. Youngdong Bridge crosses the Han River and connects north Seoul (old Seoul) and south Seoul (new Seoul). The Han river, like the Thames in London or the Seine in Paris, runs through the heart of Seoul.

Page 79: The United States invaded Iraq on March 19, 2003.

Page 80: Brothers staring at one another for fifty years refers to the DMZ between North and South Korea.

Page 108: Sansung-dong is a rich residential district in Seoul, much like Park Avenue in New York City,.

About the Author

Moon Chung-hee, one of the most celebrated poets living in South Korea today, was born in 1945 in the southern part of the Korean Peninsula and raised in Seoul. Her literary career began during her high school years, when she won first prizes in numerous literary contests Since her professional literary debut in 1969, when she published her award-winning poems in *Wolgan Literature*, Moon has published eleven books of poems including *Wild Rose, For Men, To Young Love, False Love*, and *A Poppy Flower in My Hair*. In 2004, some of her work was translated and published in English in the United States by Hwaks Publishing in a book titled *Windflower*. She has received prestigious poetry awards including the Sowol Poetry Prize, the Chung Ji-yong Poetry Prize, and the Contemporary Literature Award, as well as several poetry awards in Europe. Her poems have been translated into nine languages including German, Spanish, Albanian and Japanese. A participant in the Iowa International Writers' Program in 1995, Moon currently holds the poetry chair at Dongguk University in Seoul, Korea and is professor of creative writing at Korea University.

ABOUT THE TRANSLATORS

SEONG-KON KIM, a translator, editor and literary critic, has translated Hwang Tong-kyu's *Strong Winds at Mishi Pass* and a collection of poems by fifty Korean poets, *A Galaxy of Whale Poems* (with Alec Gordon). He has also co-authored *Simple Etiquette in Korea* (with Yi O Young) and co-edited four books in English: *Cultural Studies in Asia, Diaspora in Korean Immigrant Literature, Korean Poetry*, and *Journey to Mujin: Korean Short Fiction*. Kim edited such prestigious literary journals as *Contemporary World Literature, Twenty-First Century Literature*, and *Literature and Thought*. Former president of the International Association of Comparative Korean Studies, Kim has taught at Pennsylvania State University, Brigham Young University, and the University of California at Berkeley. He was Dean of the School of Language Education at Seoul National University.

ALEC GORDON, a poet, translator, and professor teaching at the graduate school of International Area Studies of Hankuk University of Foreign Studies, studied at the universities of Durham, East Anglia, Leed, and Warwick in England. He has taught cultural studies, language and literary studies, and sociology in a number of different countries including England, Belgium, France, Hungary, and South Korea. He was a visiting scholar at the Institute of Historical Research in the School of Advanced Study at London University. He co-edited *Cultural Studies in Asia* and co-translated *A Galaxy of Whale Poems*. He is presently writing a book of essays on translation, philology, and language.

THE KOREAN VOICES SERIES

White Pine Press launched the Korean Voices Series with the mission of developing and making widely available a comprehensive selection of Korean literature, both historic and contemporary. Support of this series by the Korea Literature Translation Institute and the Daesan Foundation is gratefully acknowledged.

One Human Family & Other Stories — Chung Yeun-hee
Translated by Hyun-jae Yee Sallee
The devastating hold the Korean War still has on ordinary citizens of South Korea is revealed in a novella and four short stories.
Volume 13   978-1-893996-87-8   232 pages $16.00

Woman on the Terrace — Poems by Moon Chung-hee
Translated by Seong-kon Kim and Alec Gordon
These lyrical poems represent poignant self-examination, evoking moments of bewilderment and hopeful resignation to the passage of time and the imprisoning conditions of her life. Her work explores the desire to escape the fetters of domesticity as a vehicle for understanding a woman's journey and her negotiations between the desire for freedom and domestic reality.
Volume 12   978-1-87399686-1   120 pages $18.00

Eyes of Dew — Poems by Chonggi Mah
Translated by Brother Anthony of Taizé
Chonggi Mah represents a unique figure in Korean poetry, similar to that of William Carlos Williams, but with a twist. While he is recognized as an award-winning poet in Korea, he has worked in the United States as a doctor and professor. Many of his poems reflect his work as a doctor and his concern with people and humanity. This first English-language edition of his work presents poems that span the length of his literary career.
Volume 11   1-893996-79-4$ 160 pages   16.00

Even Birds Leave the World — Selected Poems of Ji-woo Hwang

Translated by Won-chun Kim & Christopher Merrill

Ji-woo Hwang's poems describe a life governed by the inescapable reality that all hell can break loose at any time. In the early 1970s, he was arrested and tortured for his anti-government activities, but by the 1980s, he was leading the new wave of deconstructionist poetry which was part of the new "rhetoric of resistance" in Korean literature.

Volume 10   1-893996-45-x   104 pages $14.00

The Depths of a Clam — Selected Poems of Kim Kwang-kyu

Translated by Brother Anthony of Taize

Born in Seoul in 1941, much of Kim Kwang-kyu's poetry is sharply critical of the abuses of human dignity caused by corrupt politics and the structural contradictions brought about by the industrialization of society. His essential concern is with the value of each individual and his struggle is to enable people to realize more clearly the social and cultural forces that today threaten their humanity. His subtle protests at the dictatorships of the 1970s and 80s were especially prized and he is also one of the first Korean poets to write on the themes now known as "ecological."

Volume 9   1-893996-43-3   160 pages $16.00

Echoing Song: Contemporary Korean Women Poets

Edited by Peter H. Lee

This first anthology of modern Korean women's poetry in either Korean or English demonstrates the originality and variety of the twenty poets, active from the 1970s to the present, whose work is presented: Yi Hyangji, No Hyuangnim, Ch'on Yanghui, Kang Ungyo, Mun Chonghui, Yi Kyongnim, Ko Chonghui, Ch'oe sungja, Kim Sunghui, Kim Chngnam, Yi Chinmyong, Kim Hesun, No Hyegyong, Hwang Insuk, Chong Hwajinm, Yi Younju, Yi Sanghui, Pak Sowon, Ho Sugyong, and Na Huidok.

Volume 8   1-893996-35-2   304 pages $18.00

Among the Flowering Reeds: Classic Korean Poems in Chinese

Edited and translated by Kim Jong-gil

The bulk of Korean poetry up until the 17th Century was written in Chinese. This anthology includes 100 poems spanning over 1000 years of poetry. "Anyone interested in tasting classical Korean poetry...cannot do better than to start with this collection."— *Multicultural Review*

Volume 7   1-893996-54-9   152 pages $16.00

Brother Enemy: Poems of the Korean War

Edited and translated by Suh Ji-moon

The poems in this collection reflect the reality of a country torn apart by war and political ideologies. The work of twenty-one poets, male and female, North and South Korean appear in this landmark anthology.

Volume 6   1-893996-20-4   176 pages $16.00

Shrapnel and Other Stories — Selected Stories of Dong-ha Lee

Translated by Hyun-jae Yee Sallee

These stories by one of Korea's most revered storytellers reflect poignantly on the everyday lives of people who find it nearly impossible to cope with the progress that is inexorably wiping out the last vestiges of the Korea they loved and knew. "Stark, challenging, memorable: the work of a superb literary talent." —*Kirkus Reviews*

Volume 5   1-893996-53-0   176 pages $16.00

Strong Wind At Mishi Pass — Poems by Tong-gyu Hwang

Translated by Seong-kon Kim & Dennis Maloney

One of the most important poets in contemporary South Korean literature, this volume draws work from three of Hwang's books.. "Paradox and mystery rest comfortably side by side in these reflective poems... Hwang's quiet discoveries...keep pulling me back...for insights as strong as any elixir." —*Pacific Reader*

Volume 4   1-893996-10-7   118 pages $15.00

A Sketch of the Fading Sun — Stories of Wan-suh Park

Translated by Hyun-jae Yee Sallee

Wan-suh Park delves into the many issues facing women in contemporary Korean society, including the desire for sexual and reproductive freedom, a redefinition of familial expectations, and the struggle for economic independence."[A] gritty, elegiac collection... Park masterfully explains life in a society in which oppression is never far from hand." —*Choice* "'Momma's Stake'...is a minor masterpiece of contemporary literature...Park has delicately calibrated both the potentiality and the price of modernizations in the lives of her tragic heroines through her beautifully crafted literary vignettes. Hyun-jae Sallee's translation from Korean to English is just about flawless." —*Multicultural Review*

Volume 3   1-877727-93-8   200 pages $15.00

Heart's Agony: Selected Poems of Chiha Kim

Translated by Won-chun Kim and James Han

Chiha Kim, first imprisoned in 1964 and sentenced to death in 1974 for writing poetry that provoked the government of Chunghee Park, won the Lotus Prize in 1975. Heart's Agony gathers poetry from all eight volumes of his work. "Kim Chiha is a virtuoso, entertaining as well as brilliant." —*World Literature Today*

Volume 2   1-877727-84-9   128 pages $14.00 paper

The Snowy Road: An Anthology of Korean Fiction

Translated by Hyun-jae Yee Sallee

This anthology of Korean fiction presents work by winners of the Korean People's Literary Award, including Yean-hee Chung, Ick-suh Yo, Bum-shin Park, Jung-rae Cho, Chung-joon Yee, and Wan-suh Park. The stories offer insight into the lives of ordinary Korean people and the impact of war on their lives.

Volume 1   1-877727-19-9   168 pages $12.00 paper